The
Picture Book
of
Stencilling

The
PICTURE BOOK
of
Stencilling

A Reference Book
of Inspirational Interiors

Jill Visser · Michael Flinn

LITTLE, BROWN AND COMPANY
Boston · New York · London

A LITTLE, BROWN BOOK

First published in Great Britain in 2000 By Little, Brown and Company (UK)

This book was designed and produced by The Stencil Store, 20-21 Heronsgate Road, Chorleywood, Herts WD3 5BN
Copyright © 2000 Jill Visser & Michael Flinn

ISBN 0-316-64289-4

A CIP catalogue record for this book is available from the British Library

Little, Brown and Company (UK), Brettenham House, Lancaster Place, London WC2E 7EN

Printed and bound in Italy by LEGO SpA

Contents

INTRODUCTION

Ifirst met with Australian musician Michael Flinn to check out an unusual fireplace in his home, with a view to using it as part of a feature I was writing for *Family Circle* magazine.

I left, two hours later, knowing all there is to know about stencils and suggested that if he wanted to transform his recently found passion into a viable business he would need a set of quality photographs and press releases. I had talked myself into a job that was to be the start of a long and productive partnership!

Gradually stencils have taken over from Michael's regular music commitments and, although he still plays with his band The Mixtures, running the ever growing Stencil Store empire now comes first.

When Michael and I worked together on our first book dedicated to stencils, called appropriately *Stencilling*, this creative form of decorating was relatively new to the British public. Now, ten years on, stencilling has become an international pastime and people are forever crying out for fresh ideas on how to use stencils in the home - *and even in the work place!*

In response to this, we have compiled a collection of pictures featuring stencils in every room of the house including best selling designs from The Stencil Store and one-off originals. While some may be familiar to you, others you'll find both refreshingly new and inspirational! More advanced 'stencillers' among you will be especially impressed by the section on 'Trompe L'oeil' stencilling where we show you how it's possible, with a little helpful advice, to create realistic impressions using special shading and highlighting techniques.

The *Picture Book of Stencilling*, as its name suggests, is a collection of photographs featuring the art of stencilling at its best. The emphasis here is on the visual impact that can be achieved by the tasteful use of colour, coupled with the application of contemporary paint techniques.

Michael and I hope you enjoy this book as much we enjoyed putting it together...

...be inspired!

Jill M. Visser

HALLWAYS

Hallways

For a lasting first impression, feature stencils in your hallway. They don't have to be large scale designs in order to make a big impact!

Halls are rarely a practical option for storage so make the most of this space for display - treat the walls as a canvas or create a gallery by using stencils to link a collection of pictures.

It makes sense to start stencilling the decor just inside the front entrance - *this will provide a taster of what lies beyond*. You might even consider using the same stencil throughout the ground floor so as to achieve continuity. Alternatively, carry the design through varying the dominant shade or tone as you progress from room to room starting with the hall. Classic style suits most hallways, but especially those in period houses although traditionally inspired motifs can look just as good in contemporary homes. For maximum effect with this combination keep the look crisp by using monochrome. There's always a vast selection of stencils available to choose from including intricate Victorian inspired stencils and curvaceous *Art Nouveau* or snappy *Art Deco* designs.

Stencils In Hallways...

Avoid borders along the length of the walls in narrow halls as this will only emphasise the *'corridor'* effect. Instead, make a feature of a stencilled mural on one wall or hang a sizeable mirror and stencil around it. Use a stencil to make a high ceilinged hall seem more welcoming.

Fitting a picture rail and running a deep border between the ceiling and the rail immediately makes the hallway feels cosier!

Create the illusion of more space in the hallway by carrying the stencils over the doors - or skim the top of the skirting board with the stencil then up around the door frame. *Cheer up 'dead end' corridors with a trompe l'oeil feature!*

Happy Landings...

Door to door designs!

When it comes to decorating priorities, landings tend to be last on the list. There's nothing better than stencilling to make the decor flow - linking room to room. This area is also the perfect place to experiment with bold colours - *do beware not to use too strong a shade where no natural light is available!* If your stair carpet has seen better days, try checking the woodwork underneath - it may well be worth removing the carpet and repainting the floor; or you could strip right back to the bare wood and stencil the risers - *stencilling across each one will make the space look wider!* Use your imagination when stencilling. Here a standard Victorian border stencil *(right)* has been transformed *(with the aid of masking tape)* to mimic some decorative ironwork simply by adding some fake vertical railings.

KITCHENS

Kitchens...

Generally the most sociable room in the house, the kitchen really does deserve a warm, inviting atmosphere and nothing achieves this better than stencilling!

Consider using a style that compliments the mood of china and kitchen accessories. Folk Art motifs of animals such as rabbits or cockerels are well suited, while geometric designs can also work well - *especially when repeated wallpaper fashion over the whole wall!*

For a more traditional and authentic country look, stencil softly with a brush or sponge to echo the style of hand-painted china. Russet tones are ideal in a country kitchen although yellow is an option for creating a bright, lively environment for everyday living. If in doubt, pick out one of the strongest shades in a fabric or tile design with which to coordinate your colours.

Earthy and spicy shades are equally suited in a town house kitchen. Experiment with hues of terracotta, ochre, nutmeg and cinnamon. Liven it up with a shock of cobalt blue or saffron. Carry the rural look through with mellow timber furniture and accessorise with wicker baskets. Stencil a dresser or chair backs using subtle wood-like colours so that the piece looks 'antiqued'.

Stencilling & Kitchen Accessories...

There may be little wall space to decorate with stencils but the potential doesn't stop at walls - use stencils to transform cabinets, revamp roller blinds even kitchen accessories like storage jars, bread bins, shelf edging. Take inspiration from Portuguese & Spanish ceramics, Mexican handmade tiles or Delft pottery. Adapt the patterns as a border repeat or copy an entire piece. Stencil on wood and cut out with a jigsaw for a three dimensional effect. Mix stencils with real objects to create an interesting conversation piece. Despite the trend for unfitted kitchens, the fitted versions still dominate the market; the more streamlined and functional they are, often the more cold and clinical - *so why not add a little warmth and vitality with stencils.*

Country Flowers & Arches

T rail country flowers, vine fruits or ivy around seating areas in kitchen/diners - make the most of arches and architectural features by highlighting with stencils. You can add new dimension to glass windows or doors by using ordinary stencil paint - just wipe off with a damp cloth and change them as the mood takes you - *use stencils to compliment a dinner party theme.*

Fruits & Flowers

Fruit is inevitably the first theme that springs to mind in this food orientated environment. Simple fruit borders featuring oranges or pears suit spartan kitchens, while tumbling bunches of grapes plus a pot pourri of fruit and flowers are the perfect companions to country style - *adding even more character to cluttered rooms!*

The Kitchen...

Making the kitchen the family activity room!

Whatever the size or shape of your kitchen, the chances are it's more than just a cooking centre. The room where we spend most hours of the day tends to be the hub of the home. It's here, when we're not preparing food, that we are either carrying out household chores, doing paperwork or just socialising with friends - *as such it requires prime decorating attention*! Also as an activity room the kitchen can often benefit from the use of stimulating colours and lively stencil designs.

BATHROOMS

Bathrooms

*Here we start and end each day...
the bathroom really deserves as much furnishing
attention as any other room in the house.*

The beauty of revamping this room is that there's so little furniture to move out! Bear in mind that bathrooms are as much about relaxing as function. When considering a stencil, be guided not only by the style of the fittings, but by the mood you wish to create. In larger rooms you can take advantage of that redundant wallspace by emulating the atmosphere of ancient Roman Baths and using some large scale stencils - *columns, balustrades and urns for example*. To make the effect more convincing, sponge a mottled pattern through the stencil to achieve a stone-like look. Team with a touch of marble - *if you don't have the real thing, fake the effect on wall cabinets or vanity units with paint*. Finally, complete the look with some classic accessories like plaster plaques and elegant sculptures.

Classical Greek to Victoriana

For those who adore nostalgia, there are masses of baths and basins to suit - from the detailed basins with column pedestals and shaped backs inspired by Victorian originals to clean-edged, stepped designs like those of the Art Deco period - *as featured in the rather masculine bathroom below.*

Note how this strong style is echoed with the angular Greek Key design in both the ceramic tiles and the stencilled border. The result is even more effective due to the clever use of this most striking black and white colour combination - typical of the era.

In contrast here, the elegant Victorian Grandeur stencil echoes the curvaceous lines of the bathroom cabinet and cane chair. The colour chosen should always be entirely appropriate to the period - *sombre shades of bronze, green or claret would be ideal!*

Sources of Inspiration

Fishes, Frogs & Aquatic Flowers...

Be inspired by the shapes and details of style period furniture. Carvings and inlay designs can often be effectively translated into stencil designs. The rug design featured in the bathroom pictured opposite was taken from Art Nouveau carvings on the centre of a mirrored panel of a wardrobe which had been fixed to the wall. Several motifs were created and used together to build up a fake rug which was stencilled in woodstains so that the grain of the timber shows through. If inspiration fails you, revert back to convention and use the aquatic location as the design theme itself, building a picture of riverside or sea creatures - this works especially well in small bathrooms over a row of tiles or even along the top of tongue and groove panelling. Choose from all sorts of designs including bullfrogs, lily pads, dragonflies, colourful tropical fish or make a border of leaping dolphins.

LIVING ROOMS

Living Rooms...

Room styles are as diverse as people's lifestyles but more often than not in this room, where people relax, a soothing rather than stimulating treatment is generally demanded. Here the most popular use of stencils is to compliment the whole scheme rather than create a visual impact in its own right. In both these rooms, the architectural and floral borders serve to strengthen the decor - *while showing that different designs can work together when a coordinating colour scheme is used to harmonise the look.*

Above, a wave stencil is the perfect partner to this classically furnished room. It provides an instant *'frame'* and helps take away from the vertical line provided by the voluminous drapes and cushion print as well as focusing the eye on the display of artefacts in the corner of the room. Left, the colourful borders at dado and along the top of the wall prove that several different designs can work together in harmony with just the main colours pulling the whole together. The stencil also serves to link separate elements of this wonderfully spacious room - *adding character and warmth in the process!*

Traditional & Modern

A surprising number of types of stencils work in traditionally furnished sitting rooms. Often the way the stencil is used and the colours chosen dictate the style of the room more than the stencil design itself. Below, the stencilled border takes on a classic feel in burgundy colourways teamed with the rope and tassel - *used in vibrant shades, the same design could equally suit a contemporary decor.*

Colouring it Softly

Where furnishings are patterned, it helps to leave some areas of wall plain. To tone the effect down use a muted palette - *but where three or more patterns are involved stick to one colour!* Choosing a shade common to each will generally create a sense of harmony.

Stencilling won't overpower a room. If there are several patterns, choose one common colour to pull it together.

These Panels Take Some Beating...

When furniture is plain, you can go to town on using stencils. For maximum impact try stencilled wall panels instead of borders. Framing these rather than taking the design to the edges of the walls ensures the finished effect is not too frantic. In busy rooms like that opposite, choose a light design and use selectively.

DINING ROOMS

The Dining Area

Whether yours is a corner of the kitchen that doubles as a homework area or a totally independent room traditionally furnished with capacious table complete with matching chairs, the dining room offers great potential for stencils. Make a dramatic entrance and exit by running large stencils along each side of the doorway.

Make a bright statement in a dull, uninteresting corner with a vertical feature stencil - like a standard orange tree in a pot.. or a Grecian urn on a stately column, spilling over with an abundance of fruit and colourfully cascading flowers.

Use stencils in the tightest of spaces and bring life to a dark or uninteresting corner!

Designer Dining...

Stencils are useful devices for visually dividing the mood of the eating section of the kitchen from the area where you work. For this application it's a good idea to use a single theme, varying the treatment in the two parts of the room by switching elements or changing colours. In a dining area that is a frequent venue for dinner parties, use stencils to reflect a moody, intimate atmosphere.

Fruit designs lend themselves perfectly to any food orientated area - *as you can see in the kitchen/diner featured opposite*. Stencil a solitary bowl of fruit behind a sideboard and enhance the fun aspect - *double up on the imagery by placing the real thing in the foreground!* Add warmth and atmosphere to a clinical kitchen/diner with fruit laden branches wending their way around the top of the room.

Metallic paint can look stunning - *especially under the flicker of candlelight!* Try gold on ivory, shimmery silver on midnight blue. Strong shades of colourwash like deep red or earthy terracotta make effective base colours. Red was often used for dining room walls in traditional French homes. Teamed with fleur de lys motifs it is a favourite choice everywhere today - *especially for more formal dining rooms.*

BEDROOMS

Bedrooms

The bedroom, of all the rooms in the house, is perhaps the one where we please ourselves the most with decor. Here we can fulfill our dreams and fantasies visually in the form of a stencil. Be inspired by the bed itself - mimic carving or ironwork forms. Don't assume a stencil needs to feature on all walls of the room. Concentrating the design on one section of the room, especially one that's not too cluttered by furniture can have greater impact. Chimney breasts are great canvases for this reason - *alternatively use elements of the design to cheer up wardrobe doors.*

Floral garlands and ribbons fit the bedroom bill a treat, especially used in conjunction with country style fabrics and furnishings. A perfect accompaniment to this look is a simple wooden floor either colour washed or stencilled. Old floors should be sanded with a commercial machine before applying the stencil design and must be sealed with at least three coats of floor varnish. Run a border stencil around the edges of the room and add a large rug in the centre or create your own rug effect with stencils. Geometric stencil designs have a place in the bedroom too particularly where contemporary bedlinens are used or a Colonial style is prevalent. In the bedroom below, the bold stencilled border is inspired by the naive African artefacts. The sharp graphic shapes together with the colour scheme give a masculine edge to the room. Take inspiration from all sorts of ethnic sources - *check out primitive ceramics, South American textiles and Aboriginal paintings.*

The bedroom is the perfect place to go to town on those unashamedly feminine schemes. Delicate stencil designs never go amiss with crisp cotton linen or lace-laden beds. The essence here is keep it all light and airy.. pick a floral that drapes, like Wisteria, or one with rampant greenery such as Morning Glories - *also scatter a few floaty butterflies between the blooms*. Alternatively take a completely different route - reproduce the delicate filigree of lace on the wall with a stencil. All these equate with a romantic and relaxing environment - *complete the look with the sheerest of fabrics at the window.*

More Rooms On Top

The beauty of stencil designs derived from ancient textiles is that they work in any room although they look their best with plain, simple pieces of furniture. These strongly defined patterns look particularly stunning stencilled in deep pigments on a light backdrop or in neutral colours on a deep coloured wall. You can never overdo florals in a cottage bedroom. If you can't find a stencil to suit, why not cut your own - *taking inspiration from a floral fabric?* Stencilled roller blinds look even more effective if part of the design is cut out with a craft knife. The resulting cutwork will resemble embroidered open threadwork allowing the sunlight to filter through.

Floribunda...

Letting the flowers flow!

For the ultimate in pretty bedrooms, hunt out the most intricate floral stencil you can find and make it look as if it's growing wildly on every available surface. The more layers the stencil has, the more true to life flowers will look - *although the more expensive it will tend to be and the longer it will take to complete!* The final look will have few bridges and resemble that of delicate handpainting.

This multi-layered stencilling is particularly effective when teamed with painted effects like washes that soften or age pieces of furniture. To achieve the best results, paint the base in a similar rather than contrasting colour to the flowers so that the design blends rather than stands out of the surface.

Rampant stencilling looks especially good framing windows, doors or decorating sloping ceilings or bedrooms. Designs that incorporate fine leaves and tendrils lend themselves to running and draping around posts or down slender legs of chairs, chests of drawers and beds.

If you prefer a simpler stencil, why not combine two or more different designs for a real country garden look? Ivy leaves, wisteria, honeysuckle and morning glory are all good choices for 'trailing'.

TRADITIONAL LIVING

Traditional Living

There's something comforting about interiors with nostalgic overtones, whether it's just a flavour of the past evident in furnishings and accessories or a full-blown scheme inspired by period decor. Stencilling can contribute greatly to the final effect giving that extra touch of tradition - *there are plenty of designs derived from original sources especially the Victorian, Nouveau and Deco styles!* These will look entirely authentic when combined with the appropriate colours - *though they can also take on an unexpected current feel using contemporary shades!*

To create a Victorian look, run the stencil at dado level on a murky colour background. Typically walls were sage green or *'sober'* yellow with brighter tones like red or mauve incorporated into added borders. The discovery of synthetic dyes in 1856 produced a range of brilliant pinks so to recreate the look of the later Victorian years, raspberry tones of colourwash are ideal. Typical shades to use on top of this are red and green - *although they should be mixed with black to achieve a muddy Victorian effect!*

Borders used vertically will often give a more formal feel to a room. Use a plumb line to ensure that you keep them straight - *space wide apart to save work, positioning mirrors and pictures between the resulting columns to add character!*

Traditional Style...

Russet and yellow tones were common in Art Nouveau and Art Deco schemes as well as blues, purples, greens from turquoise to pale jade and mint to sharper lime. Along with these plenty of neutral tones - white cream and beige featured heavily. When it comes to motifs there's nothing more appropriate for traditional living than an abundance of flora & fauna reminiscent of the style of William Morris. But stencilling is not all about borders used in the conventional way. Stencil a floral flourish above the bed over an arch to give a touch of tradition or run stripes vertically to give added height.

You don't need a period house for old favourites like fleur de lys to work either. Derived from a lily shape, its strong outline makes as simple yet stunning stencil design that lends itself to many applications *(as shown opposite)*. Classic columns, coupled with cherubs, evoke Greco-Roman opulence or Regency & Empire interiors. Perfect for bathrooms and halls *(or even bedrooms)* these classical relics of the past work best in larger rooms or open spaces, teamed with marble, mosaics and plenty of greenery.

THE NURSERY

Page: 75

Nursery Style Stencils...

From the time their eyes can focus efficiently, babies thrive on visual stimulation and stencilling provides the perfect opportunity to create a fun environment from which they can learn about colours and shapes. The added bonus of stencilling a child's room compared with wall covering is that it is easily changed without much mess and when they grow out of teddy bears or dinosaurs it's easy to replace them with more sophisticated designs.

A wall in a child's room provides the perfect canvas for a stencilled mural.. build up a picture design from individual stencils.. try a woodland scene complete with forest flora and fauna.. toadstools, butterflies and fairies or a seascape with crashing waves, tropical fish or leaping dolphins plus a shipwreck and a treasure chest.

eenagers won't need any encouragement to design their own rooms and will get satisfaction from the versatility and scope of stencils. Encourage them in their own creativity. Painted bands or blocks of colour make a vibrant backdrop. For a professional finish the area should be planned out before diving in with the paintbrush and it's advisable to use masking tape used as a straight-line guide. In this youngster's bedroom *(left)* the stencilled sun and moon introduces a mystical theme while shades of lilac ensure femininity.

FLOORS

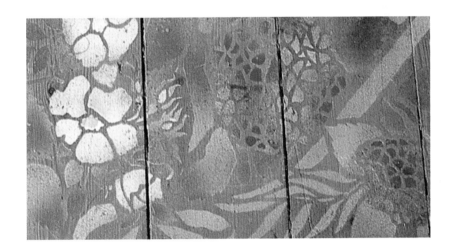

Floors & Stencils

Stencilled floors can look stunning and are a practical option in high traffic areas like halls, stairs and living areas. Wooden floorboards need to be stripped with an industrial sander back to their original state before stencilling then need to be sealed with at least four coats of polyurethane varnish, thinning each one down with one third white spirit and lightly sanding down between each layer to key the surface for the next coat - it's a good idea to sand down lightly and re-apply a fresh top coat of varnish every year!

Floor Plans...

If the thought of painstaking preparation doesn't appeal to you, fix hardboard instead as a base for painting and stencilling of floors - *you'll find it's quicker and creates much less mess too!*

A mottled paint effect like sponging in a neutral colour makes a soft backdrop. Again at least four coats of polyurethane varnish will be required for protection. Stairs lend themselves to stencilling: use one motif on each tread or riser. Alternatively, give the impression of a *'carpeted'* floor by running two parallel borders up each riser and along each tread, from bottom to top.

A bordered stencil design is often a good compromise in rooms where design is welcome but a fussily patterned carpet would be too much (see above). Another solution is to put together a collection of stencil designs to create the impression of a rug in the middle of a room (see left).

Faking it can be fun!

Before deciding how to stencil the floor, consider its shape and where furniture will be positioned. Stencilling an all-over geometric pattern works best in a room that is minimally furnished - *a large square or oblong area like a hall with few alcoves or narrowing corridors*. In an unusual shaped room it's best to use a stencilled border instead, running it near the edge of the room and following the contours. Another good solution is a collection of stencil designs put together to give the impression of a rug in the centre of the floor. You can even add realism with a painted fringe at either end *(done freehand)* or by adding a curled corner as in the picture below. With any stencilling project, the design of the stencil should always be in keeping with the mood of the room's decor

- *the beauty of stencils is that virtually any shape can be created to suit the specific furnishings!*

In the bedroom pictured above, an oriental stencil design has been inspired by the black lacquered bed and serves to create a link between this dominant piece of furniture and the rest of the room. If you need inspiration for your floor design, use any patterned floor covering as your reference. Take ideas from ancient mosaics, Persian and Chinese carpets.

The crucial move is to try out shapes on paper first *(arranging them on the floor initially)* to get the scale and position correct before you start cutting the stencils. On stripped wood floors it's important to get it right first time - *unlike with walls, you can't paint out mistakes and start again!*

TROMPE L'OEIL

TROMPE L'OEIL

Trompe l'oeil effects are sometimes so close to the real thing that it's difficult to tell the real from the fake! (Literally translated it means 'trick of the eye').

Some stencil designs lend themselves readily to create this three dimensional finish but most can be made to look more realistic by the introduction of highlights and fake shadows in the appropriate places. It's easy to create the look of dimension in an object by brushing a darker tone of the stencil paint around the edge of the stencil. Determining where the shadow would fall on a stencilled object is best judged by holding a hand up to the wall to be stencilled.

To mimic the shadow that is cast, a greyish wash can be applied in roughly the same position as the real shadow *(the strength and consistency of colour should be close to that of strong coffee).* A mixture of black and brown paint *(together with a little water)* should do the trick!

Is seeing believing?

Add more water if the colour appears to be too dark or add a touch more paint if it's too light. Always blot the brush on paper - *it's important not to apply the dilute paint too wet!* Using this mixture and an angled paintbrush, follow the shape of the object. Highlights should be placed on the opposite side to the shadows as this would be the direction of origin for any light source.

For optimum reality, imitate the effect of light falling onto an object with streaks of white paint on the stencil.

The Perfect Backdrop...

Three dimensional objects look best when they are stencilled as if *'sitting'* on a real surface rather than *'floating'* in the middle of a wall.

To achieve this, the stencil should be butted as close as possible to a skirting board, worktop, furniture surface or shelf. Alternatively an *'imaginary'* surface can be painted in. Use masking tape as a straight-line guide and brush paint in horizontal strokes - *take care not to make the colour too strong!*

You can make objects look even more effective simply by combining your finished stencil creations with another trompe l'oeil stencil and by adding some real objects. Add quirky touches of reality like fine lines to represent cracks or flaws in a pot.

Perspective comes into the equation when working in three dimension - *make one stencil look just like it's behind another by making it paler in colour and relatively smaller!*

TROMPE L'OEIL

Add dimension to narrow corridors by building up a complete scene or mural. Bear in mind that stencils of stonework and architectural mouldings look especially good when done in three tones of a single colour, working each layer slightly deeper than the previous overlay. To create the impression of natural texture use a dry brush to stipple the colour - wipe off any excess

paint on a kitchen towel. Dab large areas with a natural sponge to achieve an overall mottled effect. Finally, when stencilling foliage, it's a good idea to keep a freshly cut bunch near to observe more closely the wide variation in tones of green that occur in nature.

FURNITURE

Furniture

A stencil can add personality to furniture. Designs can be used to enhance the beauty of a chair, table or chest or even transport it into a different era. Conjure up naive charm with folk art motifs; add a touch of Chinoiserie with exotic oriental flowers. Colour can go a long way to capturing a mood - lilies or roses stencilled on a black background will give a look reminiscent of Japanese lacquered furniture while changing the accessories like door handles or drawer knobs on the stencilled piece also makes a considerable difference. Shaping with a jigsaw and adding wooden mouldings will transform the finished

effect too. For this reason a relatively inexpensive basic chest or cupboard made out of M.D.F. can look like a classic craftsman made 'one off' when painted, trimmed and stencilled. The screens in these pictures and the chair below, have all been made in this way.

It's tempting to decorate each drawer of a chest with miniature stencil designs scattered around each knob or handle; but if the fronts are flush, one stencil continuing over the whole area across the gaps will make more of a design statement.

Choose a design that is in proportion to the overall area that is to be stencilled - paying particular attention to corners - always mitre them for neatness!

reate a feature out of plain shelves with a stencil. First add a piece of timber to the front *(this will increase the appearance of depth and make them more chunky)* then add a border design *(geometric patterns lend themselves to this treatment).*

In some cases it is important that the choice of stencil should compliment the shape of the piece. On the table *(left)* a Latin script stencil suggests this is a serious piece of furniture with a function; whereas the delicate floral stencil rambling around the perimeter of the circular table *(below)* enhances the pretty shape and reveals the decorative potential of this simple piece of furniture.

After stencilling... it's important always to apply a few coats of polyurethane varnish to table tops to protect the painted finish - allow each coat to dry before applying the next!

FABRICS

Stencilling & Fabrics

Deciding on fabrics to team up with stencilled walls isn't always an easy task. When in doubt stencils can always be used to compliment pelmets, curtain edgings or even a full expanse of curtains.

Be guided by the degree of pattern in a floor covering or upholstery - *if these are relatively plain, you can make it as enthusiastically stencilled as you like; if the rest of the decor is fairly busy, keep it understated!*

Plain cushions and lampshades present further opportunities to add individuality by using stencils. Avoid long continuous designs around lampshades - *it's tricky to cope with running them around a curved shape!* Short runs or small motifs are best.

When stencilling cushion covers, slip a piece of card inside between the layers of fabric to prevent the paint seeping through the cloth.

Roller blinds are ideal for stencilling too - *they have less area than curtains and they're flat!* Not only are they easy to work with, but the complete design shows when they are pulled down - *one strong motif is often more striking than an 'all-over' design!*

OBJECTS

Making a feature of objects...

Some objects like trinket and jewellery boxes cry out for stencilling - other applications are less obvious. Use stencils where a printed form of decoration might be used; stencil on wood in tones of brown to give the impression of marquetry, or substitute painstaking handpainting for the easier alternative on the metal watering can shown below. Stencilled picture frames look particularly effective - although it's easiest to work on a broad flat frame rather than mouldings and it's important keep the design simple so as not to detract from the picture

being displayed. Use stencils to surround a framed picture or clock. You can also stencil ceramics - *strictly for decorative use only and remember that china should not be subjected to frequent washing and of course paint should never come into contact with food!* The cleverest form of stencilling by far is a stencil of an object itself that is so close to the real thing that it's difficult to tell them apart - *spot the cheat above!*

ARCHITECTURAL FEATURES

Traditionally, wooden mouldings have been used to add dimension to plain walls - *but stencils can easily be used instead!* Replace picture rails or cornices with a bold stencil and it will serve as an alternative means of breaking a large wall up into separate areas. A stencil following the line of a dado or picture rail also reinforces the effect. In a period house, choose a design that's in keeping with the style - *a solid border design rather than a free flowing floral!* Make use of stencils to alter the apparent proportion of a room. A border, run three quarters the way down the wall or further, will change the eye level and make a high ceilinged room look less imposing and more cosy. Stencils on the ceiling will achieve this lowering effect too *(although it's difficult to achieve).* A platform type ladder is almost essential to do this - *and you will need to lie on your back or risk a stiff neck!*

Ceilings, like floors, need careful planning - measure the area first and work out the plan on graph paper so that the design is well proportioned - *don't plan an entire design around a central light fitting assuming it is the centre of the room!* There are circular stencils especially designed to mimic the look of ornate ceiling roses. Stencilled pictures worked directly on the wall can also be fun - *but it's always important to select a subject that looks like a typical still life with many parts and intricate in design!*

The more overlays, the more realistic and hand painted it will look. Stencil a fake frame around it, creating the shadow of the mouldings - using the 'light and shade' technique *(see the Trompe L'oeil section - starting on page 89).*

How to Stencil

Here a Stencil...

For a lasting first impression, feature stencils all over. Create a stone effect on wood - like this mosaic on bathroom vanity units where silver metallic paint adds lustre to a 3D stencil.

Professional Tips

You can tackle any new project with confidence with a little expert advice.. and perhaps save yourself some trouble too!

To get the full potential from a stencil, it's best to experiment. Stencil on spare paper before you tackle the surface - lining paper is ideal. To build up borders, combine different shapes; flip motifs over to make a mirror image of the design and make an entirely new pattern from the two together.

It's important not to use too much paint - excess paint should be wiped off using a kitchen towel *(with too much it will creep under the stencil and smudge)*. Colours need not be kept strictly separate. Overlapping edges of colours will add shading and depth.

Mixing paints will create different shades but care should be taken where a second mixed batch may be needed - *it may be difficult to achieve exactly the same shade twice!*

As you can see, there are far more possibilities than straight borders - even in instances where the stencil is straight and regular. Individual motifs can highlight anything in a room - use flourishes over pictures, in the centre of an alcove; on panels of doors.

For best results, keep one brush to one colour and wash in hot soapy water after use. When taking a break from the stencilling project, cover the brushes with cling film to stop them drying out and getting hard.

There's no need to clean a mylar *(plastic film)* stencil after each use but if the build up of paint becomes excessive it can spoil the edge of the design. In this case, soak stencil in warm soapy water and use a scourer.

Mistakes needn't be a disaster as stencilling is not meant to be perfect but a damp cloth will eliminate the worst if used immediately.

To stencil fabric, work on a hard floor or a large table. To safeguard against paint seeping through the fabric, cover the surface with lining paper first. Then lightly coat the paper with spray adhesive or tape fabric to table to stop it moving. Avoid creases and make handling easier by draping the stencilled part over a chairback as you work on the next section.

To create an aged effect on stencilled furniture or floors, rub down with a medium grade sandpaper after you've stencilled your design.

If you decide that a stencil is too bright when you've finished, you can knock back the tone subtly by washing over the whole wall with white colourwash.

You can dictate an entire mood of a room just by the colour of your stencil. Even a classic design can look contemporary in minimalist schemes with strong colours. Stencil in claret and gold for a traditional effect or try cobalt blue, jade green, yellow or tangerine for a bolder look.

Stencilling works very well on glass though it's not a permanent solution - you can stencil a glass door or window as a temporary decorative effect using standard stencil paints. They can easily be removed with soapy water or with a proprietory window cleaner.

Taking Inspiration

Where every picture tells a story...

Choose the best stencil style for the mood you want the room to portray. It's not vital that you slavishly follow the character of the house; remember that if there's little there to start with, stencilling can start off a theme. You don't need a 1930's semi to use an Art Deco design or a country cottage to use a country rose.

Colours can dictate a mood as much as the type of stencil used and stencils can look completely different worked in different colour combinations. Take care to select the most suitable media. For bold looks you just can't beat paints. Kitchens and dining rooms benefit from strong colour but for bedrooms and living rooms a more relaxed environment is what we generally look for and here light is necessary for reading - *so think twice before painting deep red!* For a soft pastel finish use Stencil Sticks.

Think carefully too about where to stencil. Look at how the stencil works with the dominant features of the room.. surround the window, add a garland over the fireplace, fill in the panels of a door. It's important not to be too rigid; half the fun is using the motifs to create a unique pattern. Experiment with shapes.. omit some of the elements of the

stencil then try using the various components of it to make a large original mural.

As a change from stencilled borders repeat a single motif all over the wall to mimic a wallpaper effect. You can let your imagination run

riot - stencilling at random to build up a unique design. Avoid the danger of going over the top by restricting yourself to one wall - a chimney breast is ideal.

The best way to tackle an *'all-over'* project is first to stencil the design on a sheet of paper - make multiple photocopies of this and use these to plan out the design by fixing them temporarily in trial positions with spray adhesive. Balancing scale is more vital than selecting the stencil design. Delicate, dainty designs that

look charming bordering a cottage bedroom can look a little lost when skimming the ceiling of a large Edwardian sitting room.

When you're stencilling around the edges of a table, door or even a tablecloth it can be better to position the stencil centrally, then fill in the corner spaces with a single decorative motif. Face the stencil inwards for a more sympathetic effect.

With just a little imagination - plus a stencil...

the possibilities are endless!

The last word in stencilling...

FURNITURE AND WOOD

Stencils are at their most effective on furniture when in proportion to the piece. When stencilling directly on wood, choose a punchy design and strong shades to be sure it stands out against the rich timber colour.

Be guided in your positioning of your stencil by the piece of furniture - preparing the wood properly first by removing all traces of grease, wax and varnish.

When using melamine, stencil as usual but when paint is completely dry replace stencils carefully over design and apply a coat of varnish to seal the stencilled area. If you intend to repaint the piece completely, rub down the surface with sandpaper, undercoat and then use an eggshell paint as a base.

POSITIONING THE DESIGN

Centralise the motif on doors or fill up sections by doubling up the design. On a narrow chair stick to using the shallowest part of the stencil singly. If stencilling the front of a chest of drawers, you don't need to limit yourself to the size of each drawer, a design can sometimes look most effective when it's running down over the gaps.

When you choose a geometric stencil like mosaic on a circular table top, don't try to work it around the curve - stencil a block of the design in the centre and fill large areas by repeating small sections of pattern.

ADDING STYLE

Update that plain piece of furniture by distressing it with paint before stencilling or add a stylish touch to standard shelving by edging with a timber batten and then stencilling it along the whole length - it's less expensive.. *and it's infinitely more colourful than traditional timber moulding trims!*

For a little extra protection on table tops, finish off with several coats of matt acrylic varnish or you can also add character by crackle glazing all over the entire stencil.

WOODEN FLOORS

A cheap and practical alternative to carpet - *stencilled floorboards!* Make sure all the sawdust is vacuumed up after sanding and before painting or you'll get a fine layer sticking to the paint. You'll need to plan it carefully first.. draw out the design with coloured pencils on squared paper. Seal the

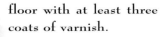

floor with at least three coats of varnish.

Before stencilling a floor design, consider the room's layout and how it is used. Restrict *'all-over'* designs to large simple shaped rooms *(no alcoves)* and furnish sparsely so the design is viewed at its best. In a smaller room a rug design stencilled directly on the floorboards can look most effective. Again finish with at least three coats of varnish to protect the completed design.

FIREPLACES

It's easy to turn any fireplace into a feature by trailing a stencil around it. Remove all traces of wax or grease before you start. You can make the most of fireplaces featuring favourite old tiles by cutting your own stencil based on the tile design and using it selectively on the wall behind. Be sure that the design complements any mantelpiece ornaments and is not merely obscured by them.

STENCILLING ON FABRIC

Use stencils to revamp table linen and soft furnishings too. For fabrics that require frequent washing, it's advisable to use fabric paint. You don't need to stencil on a cream background - any plain colour will do, but test first to make sure that the colour shows.

A roller blind is often perfect for stencilling. It's not only flat and rigid but it's also a nice size of surface to tackle. To stencil a deep border along the edge, you need to order a made to measure blind. The rod should be positioned several inches from the base. You can create an effective cutwork broderie effect by cutting some parts out. Use a sharp scalpel for this - *but don't overdo it or the blind will lose its stiffness and curl up.*

Try creating an original cloth floor mat from canvas or coloured tarpaulin covered with several layers of white emulsion paint. A commercial rug design can be used as a handy source of inspiration.

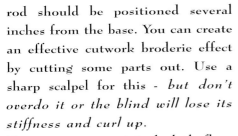

STENCILLING ON TILES

Give old tiles a facelift - *painting and stencilling them is the ideal solution.* It's always vital to prepare thoroughly for the best results. Wash tiles down and leave to completely dry, then rub over with methylated spirits. Paint directly with eggshell paint and leave for a few days until totally dry and hard before you stencil. It's best to seal with a coat of good polyurethane varnish for added protection. Simply wipe gently with a damp cloth to clean. If you are stencilling on new glazed tiles use ceramic paint - *although it can scratch off it can be easily and quickly replaced.*

Fake tiles are a clever alternative.. to create a tiled effect, first divide the area up into six inch tiled squares using pencil lines - *cheating if it doesn't quite divide exactly.* Use the motif inside the grid.. follow existing tile patterns. Finish by outlining with a permanent pen to represent grout lines and varnish on top.

STENCILLING AROUND PICTURES

Use a stencil around flat picture frames or as an internal border on the recessed picture mount. Gold stencils looks particularly distinctive in this instance. Plain glass clip frames are cheap solutions to hang prints but are sometimes lacking in personality. Add your own touch with a stencil. Adapt the design according to the print, it's important to complement rather than fight with the picture inside. Basic shapes work best for this, try a geometric border at right angles at each corner on the wall behind the picture or stencil a surround directly on the card mount. For a more traditional look, stencil a ribbon and bow on the wall above the picture. Do this en masse and build up a Print Room effect.

STENCILLING CAN BE FUN - *AND IT'S EASY!*

HOW TO... **STENCIL** *- with Stencil Paints...*

STEP ONE

Holding the stencil firmly, gently push out the pre-cut sections of the design with a pencil or your finger. *(Only applies to some stencils as most are ready to use).*

STEP THREE

Shake pot then open.. using the pot lid as a palette, pick up a little paint on the tip of the stencil brush.
Do not overload brush as excess paint can risk smudging.

STEP FOUR

Wipe off excess paint on kitchen towel. Then using a circular or stippling motion, apply the paint over the design.

STEP TWO

Attach stencil to surface with strips of masking tape or Stencil Mount, applied lightly. *(See step one sticks).*
Tip: *always try out designs first on spare paper!*

STEP FIVE

Remove stencil carefully - replace stencil as necessary and repeat to make a continuous border. Bend stencil into or around any corners to continue the design.

JUST FOLLOW THESE SIMPLE STEPS...

HOW TO... STENCIL *- with Stencil Sticks...*

STEP ONE

Spray reverse of stencil with a light, even coat of Stencil Mount. Allow to go tacky, Place stencil on surface.

STEP TWO

Using the stencil as a palette, rub the Stencil Stick onto a blank area away from the cut out sections.

STEP THREE

Using a circular motion load the colour onto the bristles of the brush. *Do not overload!*

STEP FOUR

Apply colour over the cut-out areas of the stencil - again in a circular motion. Peel off stencil - repeat process.

Some Useful Tips:-

- To achieve an aged or distressed finish on walls or furniture, wash over the completed stencilling with Stonewash White Colourwash.

- When stencilling fabric, you will need to apply Stencil Mount more liberally to ensure that the stencil does not slip while are you working.

- Always keep a damp cloth at hand to wipe off any mistakes. (For Stencil Stick errors use a cloth dampened with white spirit).

- You can use either Stencil Mount or masking tape to position a stencil to most surfaces - *you should always read the instructions carefully!*

Featured here are Stencils from the Stencil Store's own **"French Style Collection"**

A tartan stencil can
add a classic Celtic touch.

Drag in blue glaze for
this striking Shaker simplicity.

Distress white wood
furniture with paint effects for a
distinctively mellow feel.

FURNITURE

Transform a plain piece of furniture
into a designer original with scumble glaze..
then add distressing for the latest finish.

Plain doors cry out for colourful stencilling..
fill the space with a bold design like this tulip stencil.

PICTURE FRAME

Boring to beautiful.. *crackle glaze!*

STENCILS

To give a piece of
furniture personality
use the entire front
as a canvas.. stencil
liberally all over
to create a unique
and original
design.

EVERYDAY OBJECTS & FURNITURE INTO BEAUTIFULLY CREATIVE, CONTEMPORARY WORKS OF ART

Use tartan in bright colours
for a contemporary look.. classic
design, modern style.

Forget about plain pine - paint effect
your kitchen accessories.

CHAIRS

Tartan in
narrow bands
adds distinction
to a chair using a
'Trompe L'oeil'
touch to mimic an
upholstered panel
and seat.

OBJECTS

Experiment with paint effects..
re-painting and ageing can add character
to a new trinket box.

ACKNOWLEDGEMENTS

Photography inevitably means long hours and much disruption especially when it involves days of preparation before the cameras come in. We are grateful to the following for their help and patience over the years:-

Donna & Leanne Flinn for suffering changes of plans and delayed dinners.

Saleena Khara for her designs, tasteful stencilling and subtle shading.

Tracy Spurling for stepping in to help out during frantic sessions.

Dee Keller of **Deesigns** for sharing her passion of stencilling and especially for her clever trompe l'oeil stencils shown on pages 88, 89 and 92-95, also the for the stencil designs we've used on opening sections.

Steve Hawkins and **Dale Cherry,** photographers, for attention to detail on extremely long days.

Annie for letting us loose in her wonderful home with pots of colourwash and stencil brushes.

Marcia Brown of **KLC School of Design** for persuading two of her talented designers **Sue Best** (Pages 56-57) and **Katy Pryce** (Page 59) to let us add our stencilling stamp on their stylish room sets.

Clive Morgan for his skillful creations in MDF and timber.

Jennie Emery for her time and expertise rustling up soft furnishings at short notice.

Inspirations Magazine for allowing us to use the Calligraphy Photographs.

Peter and **Pam Lennon** of **Chess Interiors** for fabrics shown on Page 113.

Suzanne Murphy for sparking off Michael's addiction for stencils in New Jersey way back in the early eighties.

Stencil Store staff for their loyalty and the customers who keep coming back.

SOURCES
All materials and tools required for stencilling can be bought from any of 20 branches of The Stencil Store nationwide *(telephone: 01923 285577/88 for nearest branch)* plus selected branches of Homebase.

WORKSHOPS
Workshops at The Stencil Store include tips on approach as well as using paint effects in conjunction with stencilling. Tel: 01923 285577/88 for details of nearest branch where workshops are undertaken.

MAIL ORDER
Mail Order catalogue from: The Stencil Store, 20-21 Heronsgate Road, Chorleywood, Herts WD3 5BN. Telephone: 01923 285577/88 Fax: 01923 285136. Or visit the Stencil Store web site at www.stencilstore.com E-mail: mail@stencilstore.com

PICTURE CREDITS

HALLS
Page 10: (bottom right) Steve Hawkins
Page 11: Steve Hawkins
Page 16: Spike Powell/EWA

KITCHENS
Page 20/21: Spike Powell/EWA
Page 22: (top right) Steve Hawkins; Design: Dee Keller
Page 23: Spike Powell/EWA
Page 24: (bottom) Jon Bouchier/EWA
Page 25: (top) Steve Hawkins
Page 27: (bottom right) Spike Powell/EWA

BATHROOMS
Page 32: Dennis Stone/EWA
Page 33: Steve Hawkins
Page 34: Steve Hawkins
Page 35: Steve Hawkins
Page 37: Dennis Stone/EWA

LIVING ROOMS
Page 45: (top left) Spike Powell/EWA
Page 45: (bottom) Brian Harrison/EWA
Page 46-47: Andreas Von Einsiedel/Stencil Lyn Le Grice/EWA

DINING ROOMS
Page 52: Tom Leighton/EWA
Page 53: Steve Hawkins

BEDROOMS
Page 56-57: Dale Cherry; Room Design: Sue Best for
                     KLC School of Design, Tel: 0171 602 8592
Page 58: Rodney Hyett/EWA
Page 59: Dale Cherry; Room Design: Katy Pryce for
                 KLC School of Design, Tel: 0171 602 8592
Page 60: Steve Hawkins
Page 61: Steve Hawkins
Page 62: Steve Hawkins
Page 64-65: Design: Dee Keller

TRADITIONAL LIVING
Page 70: Di Lewis/EWA
Page 72: Dennis Stone

THE NURSERY
Page 76-77: Steve Hawkins
Page 79: Steve Hawkins

FLOORS
Page 82: Brian Harrison/EWA
Page 83: Gary Chowanetz/EWA
Page 84: (top right) Michael Dunne/EWA
Page 85: (bottom left) David Cripps/EWA
Page 85: (top right) Huntley Hedworth/EWA

TROMPE L'OEIL
Page 88-95: Steve Hawkins; Design: Dee Keller

FURNITURE
Page 100: Courtesy of Inspirations Magazine

FABRICS
Page 104: Spike Powell/Erica Murphy/EWA
Page 105: (top) Courtesy of Inspirations Magazine

OBJECTS
Page 108: Steve Hawkins
Page 109: (top right) Steve Hawkins; Design: Dee Keller
Page 109: (bottom right) Courtesy of Inspirations Magazine

ARCHITECTURAL FEATURES
Page 112: Jon Bouchier/EWA
Page 113: (top right) Steve Hawkins
Page 113: (bottom left) Steve Hawkins

HOW TO STENCIL
Page 116-119: Steve Hawkins
Page 120-125: Steve Hawkins/Dale Cherry

INDEX OF MAIN REFERENCES